A SWEET YEAR

A Sweet Year

A Taste of the Jewish Holidays

Mark Podwal

A Doubleday Book for Young Readers

A Doubleday Book for Young Readers
Published by
Random House Children's Books
a division of
Random House, Inc.
New York

Copyright © 2003 by Mark Podwal

*This book is published in conjunction with Mark Podwal's
exhibition "A Sweet Year," The Ruth Youth Wing Library,
The Israel Museum, Jerusalem, autumn 2003.*

Visit us on the Web! www.randomhouse.com/kids
Educators and librarians, for a variety of teaching tools, visit us at
www.randomhouse.com/teachers

LIBRARY OF CONGRESS CATALOGING-IN-PUBLICATION DATA

Podwal, Mark H.
  A sweet year : a taste of the Jewish holidays / Mark Podwal.
     p. cm.
Summary: Pictures and easy-to-read text introduce Jewish holidays, focusing
on the foods associated with each.
  ISBN 0-385-74637-7 (trade)— ISBN 0-385-90869-5 (lib. bdg.) 1. Fasts
and feasts—Judaism—Juvenile literature. 2. Food—Religious aspects—
Judaism—Juvenile literature. [1. Fasts and feasts—Judaism. 2. Food—Religious
aspects. 3. Judaism—Customs and practices.] I. Title.
BM690.P64 2003
296.4'3—dc21

                                                              2002155442

The text of this book is set in 13-point Bembo.
Book design by Trish Parcell Watts
PRINTED IN CHINA
August 2003
10 9 8 7 6 5 4 3 2 1

For Peter, Eileen, Debora, and Suzanne Lehrer

The Jewish year is blessed

with many holidays.

And each holiday has its special food.

Some foods celebrate a season.

Others are reminders of long-ago miracles.

A few are even said to bring good luck.

So that the new year will be sweet,

an apple is dipped in honey on *Rosh Hashanah.*

Fruits are eaten, such as the pomegranate,

said to have 613 seeds.

Just like the 613 commandments of the Torah.

Stale bread crumbs, a symbol of the old year's

bad deeds, are tossed into a river.

Washed away forever.

The tenth day of the new year is *Yom Kippur.*

It is a day of fasting and prayer,

asking forgiveness for mistakes.

Before the fast begins, *challah,*

the bread for holidays, is eaten.

Instead of being braided, as for the Sabbath,

it is made into special shapes.

A ladder made of bread helps prayers reach heaven.

A bread key opens heaven's gate.

Sukkot recalls years long ago

when the Jews wandered the Sinai desert.

For eight days, meals are eaten in the *sukkah,*

a hut that lets the stars shine through.

Autumn fruits dangle on strings,

sweetening the air with enticing smells.

Some say that very late

on the last night of *Sukkot,* the sky opens.

And a wish made at that moment will come true.

Round and round the synagogue

children wind on *Simhat Torah*.

Waving paper flags topped by an apple

and a lighted candle.

The year's weekly readings of the Torah are finished.

And right away begin again.

Round carrot slices. Round sandwiches.

Round the synagogue seven times.

Everything round is a reminder

that the reading of the Torah has no end.

Brightening winter's long nights,

Hanukkah lights sparkle in windows.

Meanwhile, potato *latkes*

and jelly donuts fry in kitchens.

Holy lights and oily tastes recall miracles of old.

Of how a little olive oil kept the *menorah's* lamps

burning in the Temple for eight days.

And of how a little army's victory over an evil king

kept the Jewish people free.

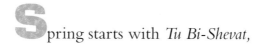

Spring starts with *Tu Bi-Shevat,*

the New Year for Trees.

Children feed seeds into the soil

to sprout in years to come.

Like the Jews who changed the barren desert

into a fruitful Promised Land.

Grapes, figs, dates, almonds, and olives:

foods named in the Bible are tasted.

And according to legend, trees kiss

and wish one another a happy new year.

Children dress in costumes on *Purim.*

Just like the beautiful Esther,

who hid her identity to save her people

from wicked Haman, who wanted to destroy the Jews.

Even *hamantaschen,* pastries shaped

like Haman's three-cornered hat,

have their secret.

Hidden inside their covers of dough

are delicious fruit centers.

Passover's special foods recall how

the Children of Israel were slaves in Egypt.

Bitter herbs for their suffering, salt water for their tears.

A mixture of fruits and nuts for the mortar used

to build Pharaoh's cities.

Most important is *matzoh,* the bread the Jews ate

during their flight to freedom.

All tasted on "a night different from all other nights,"

at a meal called the *seder.*

Shavuot celebrates the giving of the Torah

on Mount Sinai.

In remembrance of how

a desert mountain once bloomed,

synagogues are filled with summer flowers,

transformed into gardens.

The Torah promised the Children of Israel

a land of milk and honey.

So cheesecakes and honey cakes,

shaped like mountains,

add sweetness to this day.

God made the world in six days.

And rested on the *Sabbath*.

Foods slowly cook on fires lit before

the Sabbath begins.

Like *cholent,* a stew of meat, beans, and potatoes.

And *kugel,* a noodle pudding.

It is said that at the beginning of every Sabbath,

two angels visit each home.

To see if it has been made ready for this holy day.

And to offer a taste of heaven.

The years begin and end and begin again.

Sweetened with raisins and shaped in a circle,

the Rosh Hashanah challah stands for time.

It goes round and round.

And there is always a chance for a sweet year.

THE HOLIDAYS

Rosh Hashanah is the birthday of the world for Jewish people. It is the day the Jewish year begins under a new moon. Sweet foods are eaten to bring a sweet year.

No sour or bitter taste has a place on the holiday table.

Yom Kippur is the holiest day of the year in the Jewish calendar. It is the day to ask God for forgiveness. Jewish people dress in white and fast all day to imitate the angels, who neither eat nor drink.

Sukkot is a celebration of autumn's harvest—grapes, olives, squash. The *sukkah* is a reminder not only of the huts the Children of Israel lived in as they wandered the Sinai desert, but also of the dwellings of Jewish farmers in the fields at harvest time.

Simhat Torah means "Rejoicing in the Torah." Round carrot slices, looking like gold coins, symbolize the Torah's great worth. Jelly apples symbolize the Torah's sweetness.

Hanukkah, the festival of lights, celebrates the Jewish victory over King Antiochus, who would not let the Jewish people practice their religion. It also recalls the miracle in the Temple when one day's supply of oil burned for eight days. Because olive oil burns brighter than other oils, it was used to light the Temple menorah.

Tu Bi-Shevat is the fifteenth day of the Hebrew month of *Shevat*. On this day, as Israel's fruit trees begin to bud, people pray for the fruit to be sweet. Some even eat fifteen different fruits in honor of the holiday.

Purim celebrates the Jewish people's escape from destruction in Persia. It is one of the most joyous holidays, with much to eat and drink. Family, friends, and neighbors send each other baskets of fruit, and charity is given to the less fortunate.

Passover gets its name from the time God "passed over" the houses of the Children of Israel when He was punishing the Egyptians. The Jewish people fled Egypt so quickly, they could not wait for their bread to rise. So they ate crisp, flat matzoh.

Shavuot celebrates spring's abundance—barley and wheat—as well as the giving of the Torah on Mount Sinai. Some say dairy foods are eaten because when the Children of Israel returned from Mount Sinai, their milk had turned to cheese. Others say the Jewish people were too hungry to cook a meal with meat, which they would have had to prepare according to the new laws they had just received.

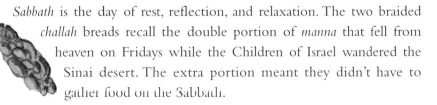

Sabbath is the day of rest, reflection, and relaxation. The two braided *challah* breads recall the double portion of *manna* that fell from heaven on Fridays while the Children of Israel wandered the Sinai desert. The extra portion meant they didn't have to gather food on the Sabbath.

AUTHOR'S NOTE

A Sweet Year originated with an invitation from The Ruth Youth Wing Library of The Israel Museum, Jerusalem. I was asked to create an exhibition centered around images of food on the occasion of the Youth Wing exhibition "Food in Art, a Matter of Taste." Rather than borrow my existing works from private collections, I conceived a new series of gouache and acrylic paintings to illustrate the important role food plays in Jewish traditions and celebrations.

Many Jewish holidays, such as Sukkot and Shavuot, began as agricultural festivals and were celebrated with shared meals. Customarily, foods were chosen for their symbolic meaning. For example, the olive oil used to fry foods on Hanukkah recalls the miraculous oil in the story of the Maccabees. At times, the holidays also took into account a food's seasonal abundance. Pastries eaten on Purim helped use up flour forbidden a month later during Passover.

The Jewish dietary laws of *kashrut* specify those foods that are permitted, or kosher, and those foods that are not. From the preparation of the foods to the blessings at the table, everything is carefully prescribed by Jewish law. Tradition holds that in days to come, even greater miracles will happen. Trees will bear fruit every day. One grape will be as large as a keg of wine. And bread will grow directly from the earth.

—*Mark Podwal*

BIBLIOGRAPHY

Klagsbrun, Francine. *Jewish Days: A Book of Jewish Life and Culture Around the Year.* New York: Farrar, Straus and Giroux, 1996.

Nathan, Joan. *The Jewish Holiday Kitchen.* New York: Schocken Books, 1998.

Roden, Claudia. *The Book of Jewish Food: An Odyssey from Samarkand to New York.* New York: Alfred A. Knopf, 1996.

Rush, Barbara. *The Jewish Year: Celebrating the Holidays.* New York: Stewart, Tabori & Chang, 2001.

Unterman, Alan. *Dictionary of Jewish Lore and Legend.* London: Thames and Hudson, 1991.

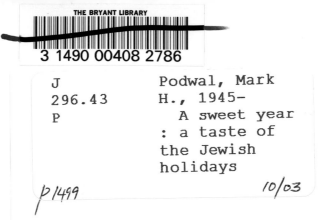